Table of Contents

W9-ANI-054

Teacher Tips

- Review instructions for students to ensure understanding of the questions.
- Encourage students to complete the answers they know how to do first.
- Create a data management word wall to reinforce math vocabulary.

Black Line Masters

Create your own worksheets using the black line masters available in this book to review, clarify or reinforce data management concepts.

Rubric and Checklists

Use the rubric and grade checklists to help monitor and assess students' learning.

Chalkboard Publishing © 2008

Data Management Grades 4-6

Reading Tally Charts

Complete.

A. Favourite Vegetable

Vegetable	Tally	Number
Green Beans	卌 卌	
Carrots	卌 卌 ||	
Spinach	||||	
Broccoli	卌		
Potatoes	卌 |||	

1. How many people chose carrots and spinach as their favourite vegetable?

_____

2. How many more people chose green beans than broccoli as their favourite vegetable?

_____

3. If 7 more people chose carrots, how many total people would have chosen carrots?

_____

4. What was the most popular vegetable?

_____

B. Favourite Sport

Sport	Tally	Number
Soccer	卌 ||	
Baseball	|||	
Gymnastics	卌 |||	
Basketball	卌	
Swimming	卌 ||||	

1. How many people chose swimming and baseball as their favourite sport?

_____

2. How many more people chose gymnastics than basketball as their favourite sport?

_____

3. If 5 less people chose soccer, how many total people would have chosen soccer?

_____

4. What was the least popular sport?

_____

MATH TALK: TALLY CHART A tally chart shows data by counting by groups of five. Each line, or tally represents 1. Once you reach a group of 5 you start another group. 卌 = 5

Reading Tally Charts

Name _____

Complete.

A. Favourite Drink

Drink	Tally	Number
Lemonade	⁜⁜ ⁜⁜ I	
White Milk	⁜⁜ ⁜⁜ ⁜⁜	
Chocolate Milk	⁜⁜ III	
Juice	⁜⁜ ⁜⁜ II	
Water	IIII	

1. How many people chose lemonade and white milk as their favourite drink?

_____

2. How many more people chose juice than water as their favourite drink?

_____

3. If 4 less people chose juice, how many total people would have chosen juice?

_____

4. What was the most popular drink?

_____

B. Favourite Snack

Snack	Tally	Number
Raisins	⁜⁜ IIII	
Fruit	II	
Pretzels	⁜⁜ ⁜⁜ III	
Cookies	⁜⁜ ⁜⁜	
Yogurt	⁜⁜ IIII	

1. How many people chose fruit and pretzels as their favourite snack?

_____

2. How many more people chose cookies than yogurt as their favourite snack?

_____

3. If 8 more people chose raisins, how many total people would have chosen raisins?

_____

4. How many people participated in the survey?

_____

MATH TALK:
TALLY CHART
A tally chart shows data by counting by groups of five. Each line, or tally represents 1. Once you reach a group of 5 you start another group. ⁜⁜ = 5

3

Exploring Tally Charts

Vivian surveyed the students in her grade to find out what type of reading genre they preferred.

Here are the results:

Fiction 30   Non-Fiction 24   Science-Fiction 15   Poetry 5   Mystery 30

Complete a tally chart to show the results.

Fiction	Non-Fiction	Science-Fiction	Poetry	Mystery

Brain Stretch: Answer the following questions.

1. How many students took part in the survey? _____

2. What kind of books did most students prefer? _____

3. What kind of books did students least prefer? _____

4. How many more students chose non fiction over poetry? _____

5. How many fewer students chose poetry than mystery? _____

6. How many students chose mystery and fiction? _____

7. Which books were equally popular? _____

8. List the genres from the least preferred to the most preferred.

_____

Reading Data Tables

10

Complete.

1. Favourite Fruit

Fruit	Number
Bananas	6
Pears	4
Apples	2
Strawberries	5
Grapes	11

a. If 2 more people chose strawberries how many total people would have chosen strawberries?

_____

b. Did more people choose pears or grapes?

_____

c. How many fewer people chose apples than bananas?

_____

2. Favourite Season

Season	Number
Winter	9
Spring	3
Summer	16
Fall	4

a. What is the least popular season?

_____

b. Which season did half of the people surveyed choose?

_____

c. List the seasons in order from the season with the most votes to the season with the least votes.

_____

3. Favourite Day of the Week

Day of the Week	Number
Sunday	8
Monday	18
Tuesday	5
Wednesday	13
Thursday	16
Friday	13
Saturday	11

a. What is the most popular day of the week?

_____

b. Which two days of the week had the same number of votes?

_____

c. How many fewer people chose Tuesday than Friday?

_____

d. Which days of the week have less than 10 votes?

_____

MATH TALK: **DATA** Data is collection of information usually gathered through observation, questioning or measurement.

Reading a Data Table

Mrs. Stephenson kept a gardener's journal to track the growth of her geranium plants. Here is the data she collected in July and August.

Plant	July	August
#1	11 cm	12 cm
#2	9 cm	10 cm
#3	11 cm	14 cm
#4	10 cm	15 cm
#5	11 cm	13 cm
#6	14 cm	16 cm
#7	7 cm	11 cm

Brain Stretch: Answer the questions.

1. What is the range of the data in July? _____

2. What is the mean height of the plants in July? _____

3. What is the range of the data in August? _____

4. What is the mean height of the plants in August? _____

5. Which plant had the tallest height in August? _____

6. What was the height of plant #4 in July? _____

7. Which plant grew the most from July to August? _____

8. Which two plants had the same height in August? _____

9. Which three plants had the same height in July? _____

10. Which plants grew the least from July to August? _____

Name _____

Bill kept track each month of how much money he collected from his paper route. Here is a list of how much money he collected during the first six months of the year.

Month	Amount Collected
January	$310
February	$298
March	$305
April	$320
May	$298
June	$318

Brain Stretch: Answer the questions.

1.	What is the range of the money collected?	2.	How much money was collected in June?
3.	How much more money was collected in June than in February?	4.	In which month was the most money collected?
5.	How much money was collected in March and April?	6.	How much money was collected altogether?

Food Cans Collected

The students at Orchard Park Public School held a canned food drive. Here are the results of their efforts.

	Week 1	Week 2	Week 3
Monday	23	40	13
Tuesday	11	44	8
Wednesday	30	28	13
Thursday	18	33	28
Friday	11	15	8

Brain Stretch: Answer the questions.

1.	What was the total number of food cans collected in week 1?	2.	What was the mode of the number of food cans collected in week 3?
3.	How many food cans were collected on the past three Wednesdays?	4.	What was the mean of the number of food cans collected in week 2?
5.	How many more food cans were collected on the Wednesdays than on the Tuesdays?	6.	During week 1, how many fewer food cans were collected on the Friday than on the Monday?

Reading a Data Table

The following data table shows the number of students who enrolled at Banting Public School during 2007 and 2008.

Grade	2007	2008
Grade 1	40	70
Grade 2	34	42
Grade 3	32	48
Grade 4	36	68
Grade 5	52	62
Grade 6	40	70

Brain Stretch: Answer the questions.

1.	How many first and third graders were enrolled in 2008?	2.	What was the increase in the number of students enrolled in grade 4 from 2007 to 2008?
3.	Which grade(s) had the most enrollment in 2008?	4.	Which grade had the least enrollment in 2007?
5.	What kind of graph would use to display this data? Explain your thinking.	6.	What do you notice about the enrollment for all of the grades from 2007 to 2008?

Name

The students at Parkdale Public School liked to volunteer at the local library. Here is a data table to show how many students volunteered over a four week period.

	Week 1	Week 2	Week 3	Week 4
Sunday	31	29	32	33
Monday	17	18	15	16
Tuesday	13	14	11	19
Wednesday	11	16	20	16
Thursday	13	20	14	16
Friday	14	14	18	13
Saturday	37	26	24	26

Brain Stretch: Answer the questions.

1.	What was the total number of students who volunteered in week 3?	**2.**	What was the mode of the people who volunteered at the library in: a. Week 1 _____ b. Week 4 _____
3.	How many students volunteered at the library for the past 4 Saturdays?	**4.**	What was the mean number of students who volunteered in Week 2? (round to the nearest student)
5.	During Week 2, how many fewer students volunteered on Wednesday than on Monday?	**6.**	During Week 1, how many fewer students volunteered on the Friday than on the Monday?

Chalkboard Publishing © 2008

Reading Pictographs

Ben conducted a survey of his cousins to see how many books they read in a month. He displayed the data as a pictograph.

Number of Books Read

Spencer	◆ ◆ ◆ ◆ ◆ ◆
Ben	◆ ◆ ◆ ◆ ◆ ◆ ◆
Madelyn	◆ ◆ ◆ ◆ ◆ ◆
Megan	◆ ◆ ◆ ◆ ◆
Michael	◆ ◆ ◆ ◆
Kaitlyn	◆ ◆ ◆ ◆ ◆ ◆ ◆

◆ = 5 books

Brain Stretch: Answer the questions.

1. How many books were read altogether? _____

2. Who read the most books? _____

3. Who read the least books? _____

4. Which two people read the same number of books? _____

5. How many books did Michael and Ben read together? _____

6. How many more books did Kaitlyn read than Spencer? _____

7. How many fewer books did Michael read than Megan? _____

8. What is the range of the number of books read? _____

9. Who read 40 books? _____

10. How many books did Madelyn read? _____

Name _____   /10

The classes took a survey of their favourite sports. They displayed the data as a pictograph.

Favourite Sports

Soccer	☺ ☺ ☺ ☺ ☺ ☺ ☺ ☺ ☺
Basketball	☺ ☺ ☺ ☺ ☺ ☺
Hockey	☺ ☺ ☺ ☺ ☺ ☺ ☺ ☺ ☺ ☺ ☺ ☺
Baseball	☺ ☺ ☺ ☺

☺ = 3 students

Brain Stretch: Answer the questions.

1. How many students took part in the survey?_____

2. What was the most popular sport? _____

3. What was the least popular sport? _____

4. How many more students chose hockey over basketball? _____

5. How many fewer students chose baseball than soccer? _____

6. How many students chose basketball and soccer? _____

7. How many symbols would be needed to show 27 students? _____

8. How many students chose basketball? _____

9. How many students chose soccer? _____

10. List the favourite sports from least to greatest.

_____

Reading Pictographs

Jane conducted a survey of favourite ice cream flavours. She displayed her data as a pictograph.

Favourite Ice Cream Flavours

Strawberry	🍦🍦🍦🍦🍦🍦🍦🍦🍦🍦🍦
Chocolate Chip	🍦🍦🍦🍦🍦
Vanilla	🍦🍦🍦🍦🍦🍦🍦🍦🍦
Chocolate	🍦🍦🍦🍦

🍦 = 4 people

Brain Stretch: Answer the questions.

1. What flavour is the most popular? _____

2. What flavour is the least popular? _____

3. How many students chose vanilla? _____

4. How many fewer students chose chocolate over vanilla? _____

5. How many students chose strawberry and vanilla? _____

6. How many students chose chocolate? _____

7. How many students chose chocolate chip? _____

8. What is the ratio of strawberry to chocolate chip?_____

9. What is the ratio of vanilla to chocolate? _____

10. How many students voted altogether? _____

Chalkboard Publishing © 2008

Reading Bar Graphs

Complete.

1. Time Spent Studying Spelling Words

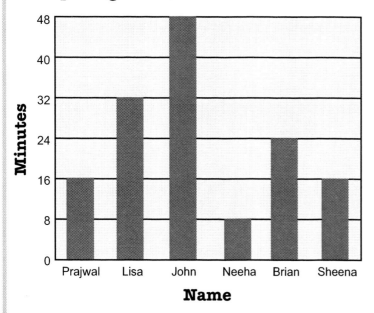

a. Who spent the most time studying spelling words?

_____

b. What is the range?

_____

c. How many minutes did Neeha and Prajwal study altogether?

_____

d. How many students were surveyed?

_____

e. How many more minutes did John study than Sheena?

_____

2. Pop Tabs Collected Each Month

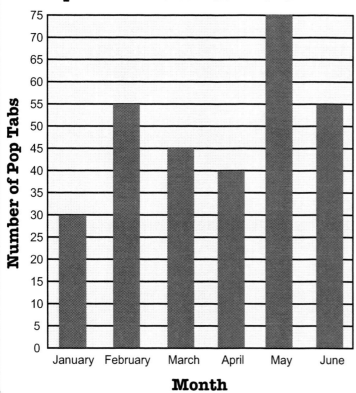

a. Which month had the least amount of pop tabs collected?

_____

b. What is the mode?

_____

c. How many fewer pop tabs were collected in January than June?

_____

d. Which month had the most amount of pop tabs collected?

_____

e. What is the difference of pop tabs collected in February and May?

_____

Reading Bar Graphs

Peter wanted to find out what kind of transportation students in his grade used to go to school. Here are the results.

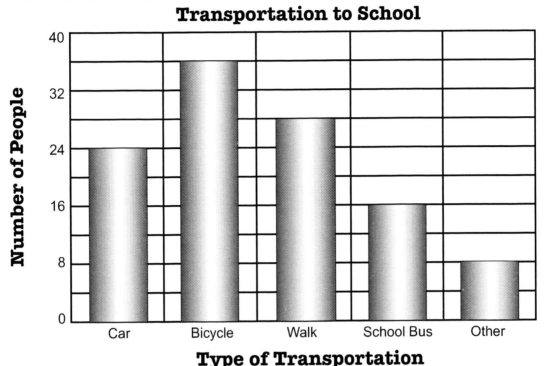

Transportation to School

Brain Stretch: Answer the questions.

1. What is the most popular form of transportation? _____

2. What is the least popular form of transportation? _____

3. How many more students walk than ride the school bus? _____

4. Did more students choose car or bicycle? _____

5. How many students ride either in a car or walk? _____

6. How many fewer students walk than ride a bicycle? _____

7. List the transportation from the transportation chosen the least to the

transportation chosen the most. _____

Exploring Bar Graphs

Josh did a survey of the colour of cars found at the Super Mart parking lot. Complete the bar graph using the data collected.

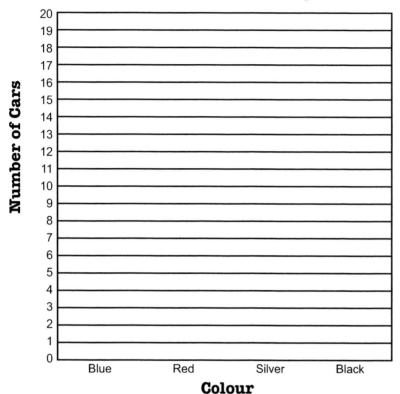

Colour of Cars in Parking Lot

Colour of Car	Number
Blue	17
Silver	7
Red	13
Black	6

Brain Stretch: Answer the questions.

1.	How many more silver cars are there than black cars?	2.	Which colour has the least amount of cars in the parking lot?
3.	How many fewer red cars are there than blue?	4.	How many cars were either red or blue?
5.	What is the range?	6.	How many more cars were needed so there would be 12 black cars?
7.	How many cars in the parking lot altogether?	8.	List the colour of car from the colour with the least to the colour with the most number of cars.

Reading Horizontal Graphs

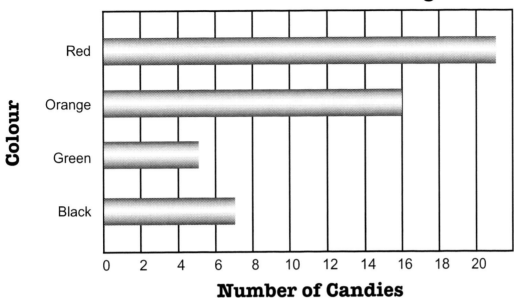

Colour of Candies in a Bag

Brain Stretch: Answer the questions.

1.	What colour of candy was there most of in the bag?	**2.**	How many candies were either red or green candies?
3.	What is the range of the colour of candies?	**4.**	What is the difference between the number of red and orange candies?
5.	How many more orange candies were there than black candies?	**6.**	How many candies were in the bag altogether?
7.	List of the colour of candies in the bag from the fewest to the most.	**8.**	If there were 2 more orange candies, how many orange candies would there be?

Exploring Bar Graphs

Karen conducted a survey on students' favourite type of music. Here are the results.

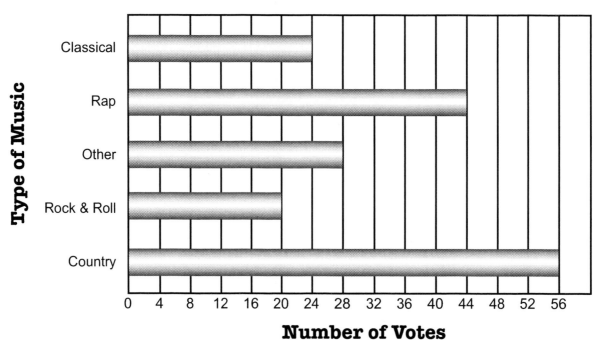

Favourite Music

Brain Stretch: Answer the questions.

1. How many people answered the survey? _____

2. What is the most popular choice of music? _____

3. What is the least popular choice of music? _____

4. How many more people chose classical than chose rock & roll? _____

5. Did more people choose country or other? _____

6. How many people chose rap or other? _____

7. If 9 more people chose rap how many
   total people would have chosen rap? _____

8. List the music in order from the music from
   the fewest votes to the music with the most votes. _____

Reading Horizontal Graphs

Spelling Test Results

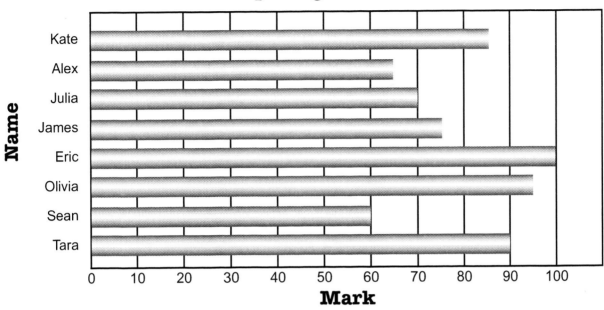

Name (vertical axis)

Kate, Alex, Julia, James, Eric, Olivia, Sean, Tara

Mark (horizontal axis): 0, 10, 20, 30, 40, 50, 60, 70, 80, 90, 100

Brain Stretch: Answer the questions.

1.	Who got 100 on their spelling test?	2.	Which student(s) got a mark between 60 and 80?
3.	What is the range of test marks?	4.	What is the difference between James and Olivia's marks?
5.	What is the mean mark?	6.	Who got 60 on their spelling test?
7.	List the names of students from the highest mark to the lowest mark.	8.	Who got 10 marks less than Eric?

Reading Horizontal Graphs

Money Spent on New Clothes

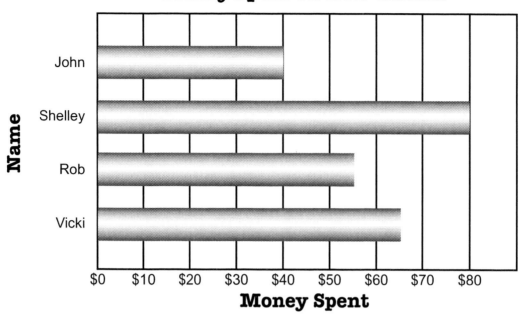

Brain Stretch: Answer the questions.

1.	Who spent the most money and how much?	**2.**	How much more money did Shelley spend than John?
3.	What is the range of money spent?	**4.**	What is the difference between what Rob and Vicki spent?
5.	How much money did Vicki and Shelley spend?	**6.**	Who spent 40 dollars?
7.	List the names from those who spent the least to those who spent the most?	**8.**	If Rob spent 10 more dollars, how much would he have spent?

Constructing Horizontal Bar Graphs

Construct a horizontal bar graph using the information from the table.

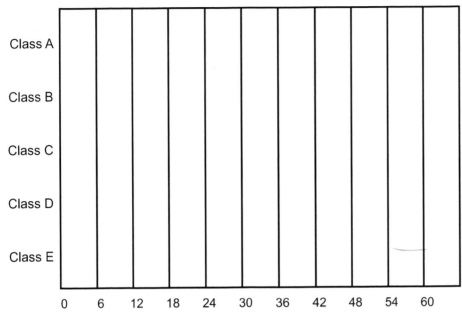

Number of Books Read

Class	Number of Books
Class A	54
Class B	42
Class C	48
Class D	36
Class E	60

Name (vertical axis)

Number of Books (horizontal axis)

0 6 12 18 24 30 36 42 48 54 60

Brain Stretch: Answer the questions.

1.	Which class read the most books?	**2.**	If each student in Class C read 2 books, how many students are in Class C?
3.	Which class read the fewest number of books?	**4.**	What is the range of books read?
5.	List the classes from the class that read the most books to the class that read the fewest books.	**6.**	How many classes read more than 48 books?

Reading Double Bar Graphs

Here is a double bar graph of how much money two classes collected for a class trip.

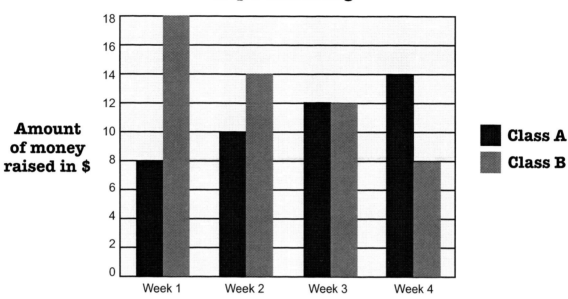

Trip Fundraising

Amount of money raised in $

Class A
Class B

Week 1 Week 2 Week 3 Week 4

Brain Stretch: Write 10 things you know from the graph.

1. _____

2. _____

3. _____

4. _____

5. _____

6. _____

7. _____

8. _____

9. _____

10. _____

Reading Double Bar Graphs

Here is a double bar graph to show how many minutes Kate and Mark spend reading each week night.

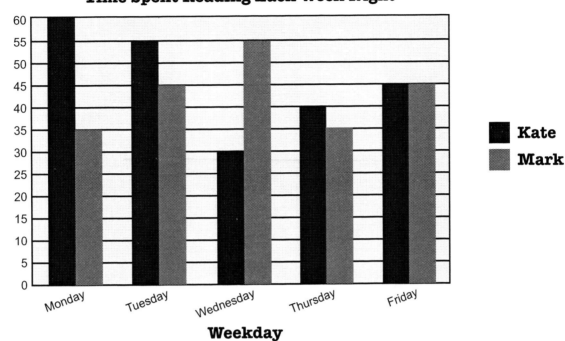

Time Spent Reading Each Week Night

Number of Minutes

Weekday

■ Kate
■ Mark

Brain Stretch: Answer the questions.

1. What is the total amount of minutes that Kate and Mark read altogether? _____

2. On what night of the week did Mark read more than Kate? _____

3. How many fewer minutes did Mark read than Kate on Monday? _____

4. How many minutes did Kate read on Tuesday? _____

5. How many minutes did Mark read on Thursday? _____

6. Who read less on Thursday?_____

7. What was the range of the minutes read by Kate? _____

8. On what day of the week did Kate and Mark read the same number of minutes? _____

9. What was the range of minutes read by Mark? _____

10. What was the difference of minutes on Wednesday? _____

Reading Double Bar Graphs

Here is a double bar graph to show how many of each colour tulip Chris and Sophie have planted in their garden.

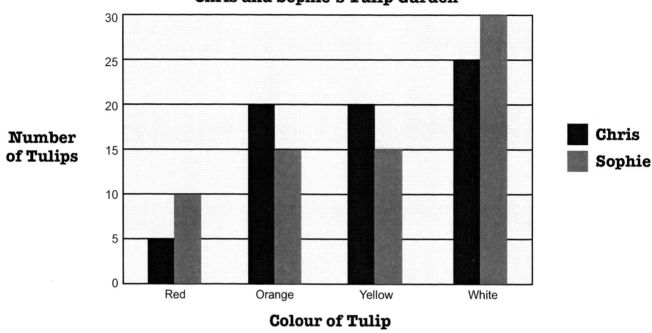

Chris and Sophie's Tulip Garden

Number of Tulips

Colour of Tulip

Chris
Sophie

Brain Stretch: Answer the questions.

1. What is the total amount of tulips that Chris and Sophie have planted together? _____

2. How many more yellow tulips does Chris have than Sophie? _____

3. How many fewer white tulips does Chris have than Sophie? _____

4. How many red tulips has Chris planted? _____

5. How many orange tulips has Sophie planted? _____

6. How many flowers has Sophie planted altogether? _____

7. How many flowers has Chris planted altogether? _____

8. Which colour tulips does Chris have the same number? _____

9. Which colour tulip does Sophie have the least? _____

10. Which colour tulip do Chris and Sophie both have the most of? _____

Reading Double Bar Graphs

10

Here is a double bar graph to show the kind of milk students preferred to drink in the cafeteria over the course of a school week.

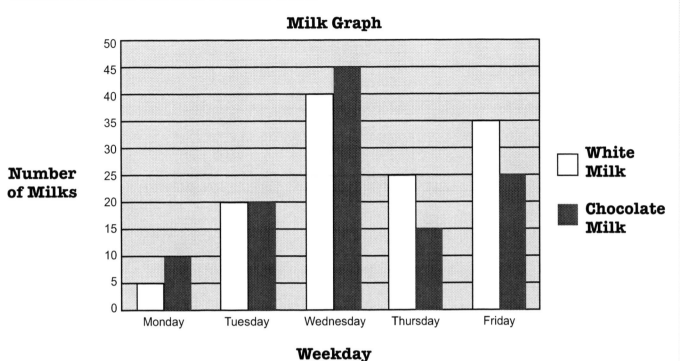

Milk Graph

Number of Milks

White Milk

Chocolate Milk

Weekday

Brain Stretch: Answer the questions.

1. How many chocolate milks were drunk over the course of the week? _____

2. How many white milks were drunk on Monday and Tuesday? _____

3. How many fewer chocolate milks than white milks were drunk on Thursday? _____

4. How many white milks were drunk on Friday? _____

5. On what day of the week was the same number of white and chocolate milk drunk? _____

6. What kind of milk was drunk more on Monday? _____

7. How many more white milks were drunk on Thursday than chocolate milks? _____

8. On what day of the week was the most chocolate milk drunk? _____

9. On what day of the week was the least white milk drunk? _____

10. How many white and chocolate milks were drunk altogether during the week? _____

Constructing a Double Bar Graph

The grade six classes were asked if they wanted to go to Ottawa for their end of the year field trip. There are 64 students in grade 6. Here are their responses.

Remember!! All the Parts of A Graph Neatness Counts!! Spelling Counts!

15

YES		NO		UNDECIDED	
Boys	Girls	Boys	Girls	Boys	Girls
16	20	4	2	4	8

A. Complete and label a double bar graph to show the data.

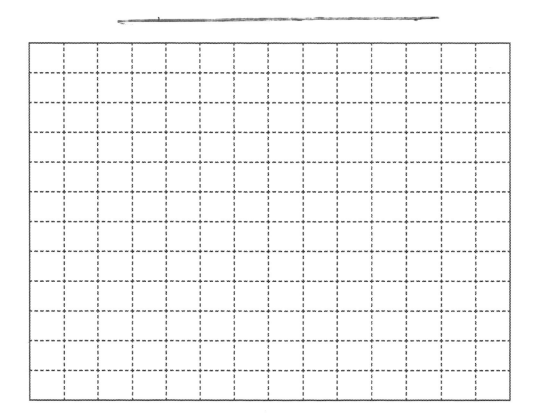

Chalkboard Publishing © 2008

Constructing a Double Bar Graph

Here is a table to show the number of points the Bears and Tigers scored during this week's soccer house league games held each recess.

Team	Monday	Tuesday	Wednesday	Thursday	Friday
Bears	15	25	30	15	10
Tigers	20	20	25	30	15

A. Complete and label a double bar graph to show the data.

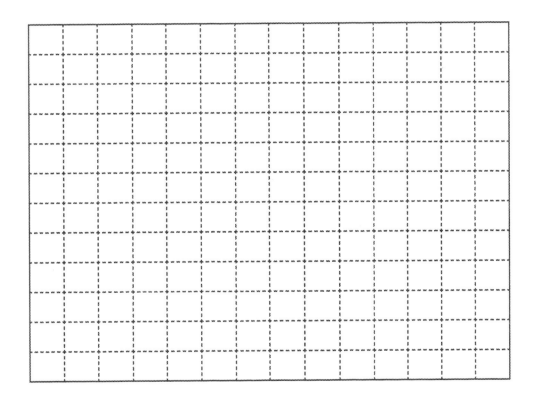

Brain Stretch: What can you infer from the graph?

1. _____

2. _____

3. _____

Line Graphs

Complete.

1. Monthly Rainfall

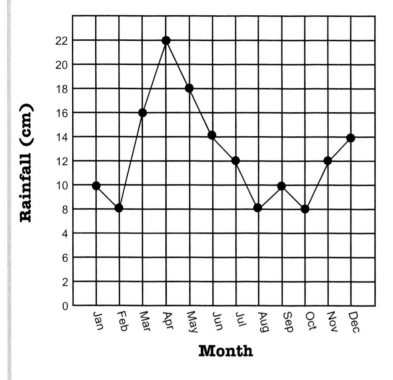

a. What was the difference of rainfall between May and February?

_____

b. Which month had the most rainfall?

_____

c. What was the range of rainfall?

_____

d. What was the rainfall in June?

_____

e. How much rainfall was there in September and October?

_____

2. Plant Growth

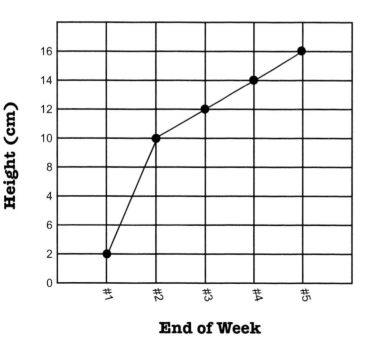

a. How tall is the plant at the end of week 3?

_____

b. What was the difference of the plant's height from week 3 to week 4?

_____

c. What was the height of the plant at the end of week 4?

_____

d. What was the range of the height of the plant?

_____

e. How much taller was the plant in week 4 than in week 2?

_____

Chalkboard Publishing © 2008

Reading Line Graphs

Elmwood Public School performed their school play for four days. Here are how many tickets were sold each night.

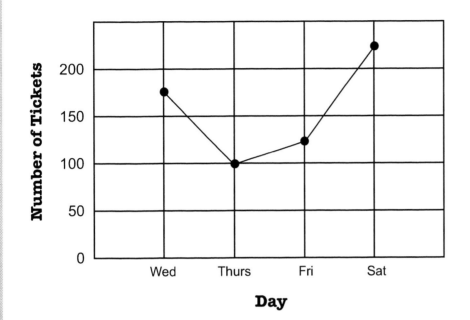

Day	Number of Tickets
Wednesday	
Thursday	
Friday	
Saturday	

Brain Stretch: Complete the data table and answer the questions.

1.	On which day were the most tickets sold?	2.	On which day were the least tickets sold?
3.	On which day was the attendance 100 people?	4.	How much of an increase of tickets sold was there from Friday to Saturday?
5.	What was the range of tickets sold?	6.	What would be a good title for this graph?

Name

Constructing Line Graphs

Complete the line graph using the information from the data table.

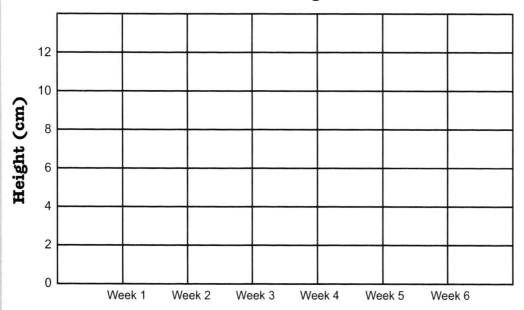

Plant Height

End of Week	Height (cm)
Week 1	2
Week 2	4
Week 3	6
Week 4	8
Week 5	10
Week 6	12

End of Week

Brain Stretch: Answer the questions.

1.	At the end of which week(s) was the plant taller than 10 centimetres?	**2.**	How much did the plant grow from the end of week #1 to the end of week #2?
3.	At the end of which week(s) was the plant no more than 4 centimetres tall?	**4.**	What was the range of the height of the plant?
5.	What was the height of the plant at the end of week 5?	**6.**	What do you notice about the increase of height from week to week?

Constructing Line Graphs

Complete the line graph using the information from the data table. Graph Oak Town's average monthly temperature for five consecutive months.

Oak Town Average Monthly Temperature

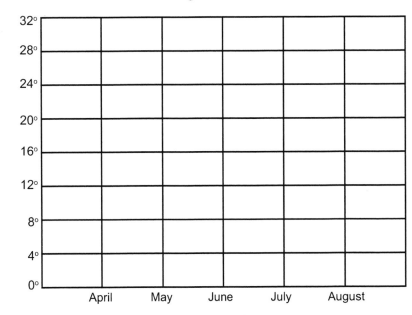

Month	Temperature in Celcius
April	12°
May	18°
June	20°
July	28°
August	28°

Brain Stretch: Answer the questions.

1.	What month had an average temperature of 18°?	2.	What was the range of temperature?
3.	What was the difference of average temperature between July and April?	4.	What was the mode?
5.	How much warmer was it in June than May?	6.	What pattern did you notice about the average temperature from month to month?

Reading Circle Graphs

This is a circle graph to show the favourite kind of farm animals of students in Mr. Turnbull's class.

Favourite Farm Animals

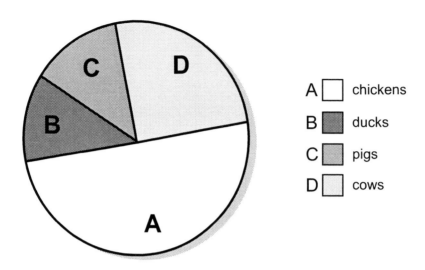

A ☐ chickens

B ◼ ducks

C ◼ pigs

D ☐ cows

Brain Stretch: Answer the questions.

1.	What was the most popular farm animal?	2.	About what fraction of students chose cows?
3.	About what fraction of students chose chickens?	4.	Which two animals together represent about ¼ of the votes?

Reading Circle Graphs

This is a circle graph to show the favourite kind of music of students in Mrs. Simpson's class.

Favourite Music

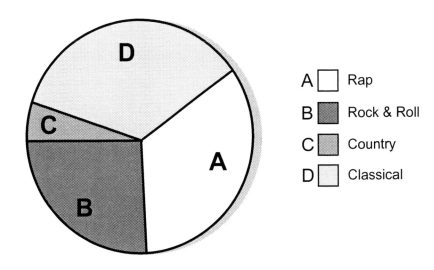

A ☐ Rap
B ☐ Rock & Roll
C ☐ Country
D ☐ Classical

Brain Stretch: Answer the questions.

1.	What was the most popular music chosen?	2.	What was the least popular music chosen?
3.	About what fraction of students chose classical music?	4.	List the music from the most popular to the least popular.

Reading Circle Graphs

There are 200 students who attend Sherwood Forest Public School. Here is a circle graph to show the students' favourite type of breakfast.

Students' Favourite Breakfast

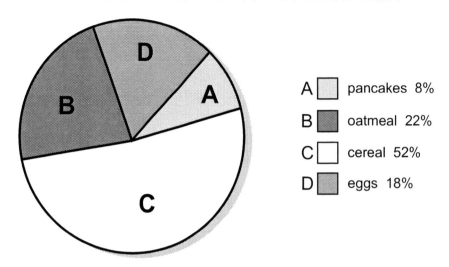

A ☐ pancakes 8%

B ▨ oatmeal 22%

C ☐ cereal 52%

D ▨ eggs 18%

Brain Stretch: Answer the questions.

1.	What fraction of the students chose cereal as their favourite breakfast?	**2.**	There are 200 students. How many students chose cereal?
3.	There are 200 students. How many students chose eggs?	**4.**	How many more students eat eggs than pancakes?
5.	What fraction of students chose oatmeal as their favourite breakfast?	**6.**	There are 200 students. How many students chose pancakes?

Reading Circle Graphs

120 students were surveyed about their favourite kind of sport. Here is a circle graph to show the students' responses.

Students' Favourite Sports

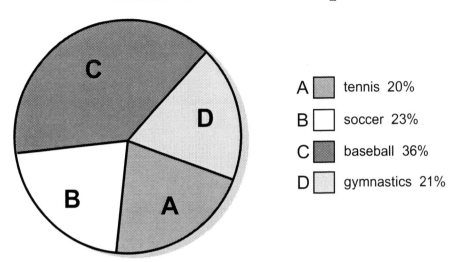

A ☐ tennis 20%

B ☐ soccer 23%

C ☐ baseball 36%

D ☐ gymnastics 21%

Brain Stretch: Answer the questions.

1.	What fraction of students chose tennis as their favourite sport?	2.	What is the ratio of baseball to gymnastics?
3.	There are 120 students. What is the number of students that chose soccer?	4.	There are 120 students. What is the number of students that chose baseball?
5.	Which sport did more than ¼ of students choose as their favourite?	6.	List the favourite sports in order from the sport with the fewest votes to the sport with the most votes.

Reading Circle Graphs

Number of Pets

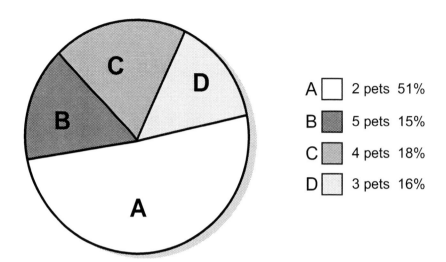

A ☐ 2 pets 51%
B ▨ 5 pets 15%
C ▨ 4 pets 18%
D ☐ 3 pets 16%

Brain Stretch: Answer the questions.

1.	How many pets do more than 50% of the people who voted have?	**2.**	What is the ratio of people with 4 pets to people with 3 pets?
3.	What percentage of people have 5 pets?	**4.**	What is the percent difference of people who have 2 pets and people who have 4 pets?
5.	What is the combined percentage of people who have 3 pets and 5 pets?	**6.**	What fraction of people have 4 pets?

Reading Circle Graphs

Transportation to School

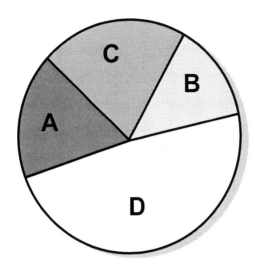

A ■ walk 20%

B □ bike 12%

C ▨ drive 22%

D □ school bus 46%

Brain Stretch: Answer the questions.

1.	What method of transportation to school do 22% of students use?	**2.**	What is the ratio of students who ride their bike to students who get a car ride?
3.	What is the most popular method of transportation to school?	**4.**	What is the percent difference of students who drive to students who walk?
5.	What is the combined percentage of students who either walk or take a school bus?	**6.**	What fraction of students ride their bike to school?

Finding Range

Find the range for each set of data. Show your work.

1.	14, 5, 21, 14, 6, 3, and 14	2.	5, 26, 21, 8, and 5
3.	20, 7, 14, 28, 14, and 13	4.	9, 10, 10, 6, and 5
5.	11, 22, 24, 13, 17, and 3	6.	2, 18, 28, 25, 17, 7, and 22
7.	13, 25, 5, 19, 11, and 29	8.	14, 14, 21, 8, and 8
9.	2, 15, 20, 27, 14, 24, and 10	10.	13, 24, 21, 12, and 10
11.	21, 5, 7, 7, 24, and 14	12.	7, 8, 10, 28, 15, 10, and 13
13.	17, 19, 16, 27, and 26	14.	16, 28, 22, 24, 25, and 23
15.	11, 2, 22, 13, 9, 19, and 15	16.	29, 14, 14, 17, 22, 3, and 27
17.	15, 21, 19, 24, and 11	18.	8, 18, 21, 11, 18, and 2
19.	20, 20, 15, 25, and 15	20.	10, 3, 16, 11, 2, 15, and 27

MATH TALK: RANGE Range is the difference between the greatest value and the least value.

Finding Range

Find the range for each set of data. Show your work.

1.	20, 15, 12, 26, and 2	2.	3, 27, 26, 25, 19, and 2
3.	23, 6, 6, 22, 17, 8, and 23	4.	10, 4, 15, 15, 2, 15, and 2
5.	28, 19, 4, 9, 26, and 28	6.	23, 23, 24, 12, and 28
7.	13, 8, 25, 23, 28, 23, and 20	8.	22, 11, 5, 14, and 18
9.	23, 12, 25, 20, 26, and 26	10.	3, 27, 15, 4, 29, and 6
11.	4, 17, 18, 21, 20, 13, and 12	12.	21, 16, 14, 19, and 15
13.	23, 7, 18, 19, and 8	14.	28, 5, 26, 14, 19, 9, and 11
15.	17, 28, 24, 19, 23, and 15	16.	11, 6, 17, 7, 16, and 27
17.	25, 16, 8, 22, and 9	18.	18, 2, 25, 20, 7, 9, and 10
19.	29, 9, 26, 6, 14, 25, and 3	20.	5, 14, 9, 2, and 20

Finding Mean

Find the mean for each set of data. Show your work

1.	**11, 13, 12, 24, and 25**	**2.**	**8, 6, 22, 4, 24, and 14**
3.	**2, 2, 7, 3, 24, 26, and 13**	**4.**	**15, 27, 11, 3, 5, and 29**
5.	**8, 4, 24, 15, 7, 2, and 24**	**6.**	**26, 16, 10, 23, and 25**
7.	**2, 7, 24, 20, and 22**	**8.**	**14, 2, 8, 21, 10, and 11**

MATH TALK:
MEAN   Mean or the average is the sum of the numbers divided by the number of addends.

Finding Mean

Find the mean for each set of data. Show your work

1.	12, 12, 11, 7, 12, 16, and 21	**2.**	19, 19, 23, 27, and 27
3.	25, 14, 9, 11, 18, and 13	**4.**	12, 3, 27, 22, 22, 3, and 16
5.	20, 12, 16, 11, and 16	**6.**	6, 6, 7, 8, 18, and 21
7.	16, 12, 8, 26, 16, 16, and 25	**8.**	5, 10, 4, 17, 16, and 2

Mean, Median, and Mode

MATH TALK:

MEAN	is the sum of the numbers divided by the number of addends.
MEDIAN	is the middle number. Find the median by ordering the numbers from least to greatest. Then find the number in the middle of the list. If there is a set of even numbers, then the median is the mean of the two middle numbers.
MODE	is the number that occurs most often.

Find the mean, median, and mode of each set of data. Show your work.

1.	13, 20, 2, 9, and 16	2.	26, 7, 7, 7, and 8
3.	25, 25, 26, 12, 12, and 20	4.	19, 18, 27, 18, and 18
5.	6, 6, 6, 5, and 27	6.	6, 24, 6, 4, and 5
7.	10, 5, 4, 6, 6, and 5	8.	19, 18, 18, 7, 21, and 7
9.	16, 8, 21, 11, 8, and 8	10.	2, 4, 2, 4, and 8

Sorting Data

1. Sort factors into the Venn Diagram, using the rules listed below.

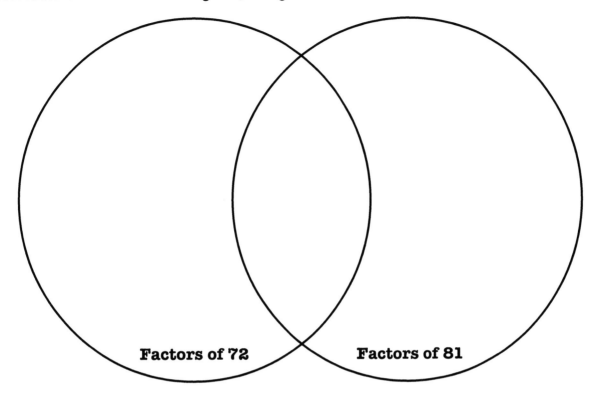

Factors of 72   **Factors of 81**

2. Sort factors into the Venn Diagram, using the rules listed below.

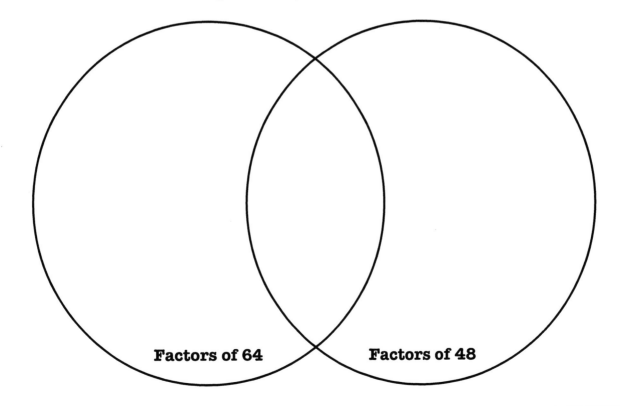

Factors of 64   **Factors of 48**

Chalkboard Publishing © 2008

Sorting Data

1. Sort factors into the Venn Diagram, using the rules listed below.

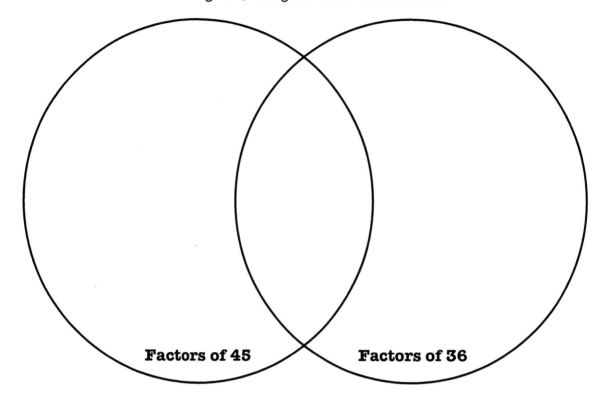

Factors of 45   **Factors of 36**

2. Sort factors into the Venn Diagram, using the rules listed below.

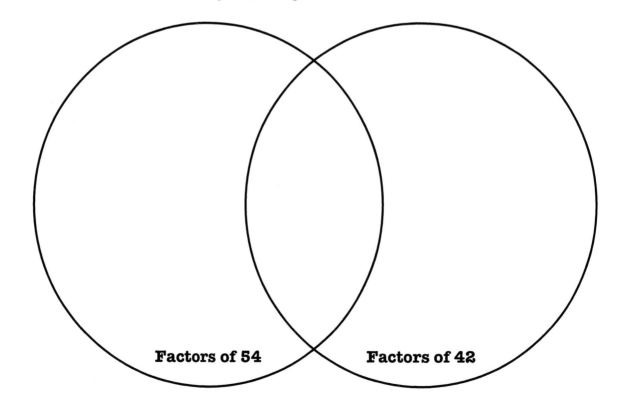

Factors of 54   **Factors of 42**

Stem-and-Leaf Plots #1 Practice

Answer the questions.

1. Find the mode of the data.

Stem	Leaves
66	5
67	4 1 2
68	7
69	2 9

2. Find the mean of the data.

Stem	Leaves
5	9 4 5 7 9 9 6
6	1 0 0

3. Find the range of the data.

Stem	Leaves
14	8 7 7
15	5 1
16	3 2
17	1 1 6
18	0

4. Find the median of the data.

Stem	Leaves
2	5
3	8 6
4	4 6 5

5. Find the mean of the data.

Stem	Leaves
1	1 3 1
2	5
3	4
4	0
5	0 7 6

6. Find the range of the data.

Stem	Leaves
13	0 9 7 2 3
14	5 8
15	4 2 0
16	9 8 9 0 4

7. Find the mode of the data.

Stem	Leaves
43	4 7 1
44	3 1 6
45	9 4
46	0
47	3 9
48	0 3

8. Find the median of the data.

Stem	Leaves
0	5 1
1	
2	
3	6 5 4
4	5

Name _____

Answer the questions.

1. Find the mode of the data.

Stem	Leaves
5	1 3 4 1 0 0 0 8
6	3 2 5 3 9
7	5 1

mode _____

2. Find the mean of the data.

Stem	Leaves
32	8 0
33	3
34	3

mean _____

3. Find the median of the data.

Stem	Leaves
6	6 7 4 8
7	6 8 4 2
8	0
9	0 7 7 9

median _____

4. Find the range of the data.

Stem	Leaves
17	8 0 1 0 5 2 7
18	1 6 1 3 2 8

range _____

5. Find the median of the data.

Stem	Leaves
11	4 3
12	3 8 7 7
13	7 3
14	2 7 1
15	9 7 8 8
16	5 8

median _____

6. Find the mode of the data.

Stem	Leaves
3	8 4 7 6
4	5
5	
6	0 3 1
7	3 3

mode _____

7. Find the mean of the data.

Stem	Leaves
0	0
1	4 1
2	0 0
3	9 6

mean _____

8. Find the range of the data.

Stem	Leaves
24	8 5 2 8
25	3 8

range _____

Answer the questions.

1. Find the mean of the data.

Stem	Leaves
3	4 6
4	
5	3 7

2. Find the range of the data.

Stem	Leaves
62	3 5
63	2 2
64	7
65	6
66	6 3
67	3 5

3. Find the mode of the data.

Stem	Leaves
16	9 6 2 2 1
17	0 1 1 4
18	3 9 6 1 4 0 7
19	7 5 4

4. Find the mode of the data.

Stem	Leaves
1	2 2 9 5
2	8 8 4 4
3	9
4	4 2 0
5	3
6	8
7	2 2 9 5

5. Find the mean of the data.

Stem	Leaves
24	0 9 8 8
25	6 1
26	9 4
27	2 3

6. Find the mean of the data.

Stem	Leaves
0	1 8 7 9 7 0 2 3
1	5 5 5 9 6

7. Find the range of the data.

Stem	Leaves
14	3 8
15	7 6
16	8
17	8 7
18	4 3

8. Find the mean of the data.

Stem	Leaves
6	0 8
7	0 1 2
8	5

Displaying Data

BAR GRAPHS

Bar graphs use horizontal or vertical bars that display data.

- Bar graphs are a good choice to display data if you want to compare data.

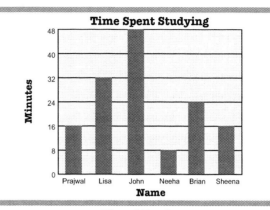

LINE GRAPHS

Line graphs use points that are joined which represent data over time.

- Line graphs are a good choice to display data if you want to show change over time.

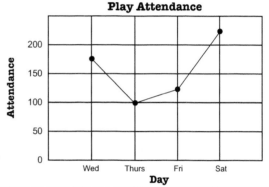

CIRCLE OR PIE GRAPHS

This is a graph in which a circle used to represent a whole and is divided into parts that represent parts of the whole.

- Circle or pie graphs are a good choice to display data if you want to compare parts of a whole.

PICTOGRAPHS

Pictographs use pictures or icons to show data and to compare information. Each picture or icon can represent more than one object. A key is used to what each picture represents.

- Pictographs are a good choice to display data if you want to compare data.

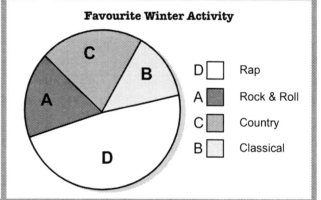

Choosing Appropriate Graphs

What type of graph would you use to display the following data?

Line Graph • Bar Graph • Circle Graph • Double Bar Graph • Pictograph

1. comparing students' favourite colours	2. showing how a person spent $100	3. comparing the number of different types of books read by two classes during the month of may
4. comparing the number of hours two different children practice piano every night for a week	5. comparing students' favourite television shows	6. showing the growth of a plant over six weeks
7. showing the price of a stock over a month	8. comparing the different kinds of birds seen in the school yard	9. comparing students' hair colour
10. comparing the height of different children	11. showing how much time a child spends their day on different activities	12. showing the snowfall for a month

Conducting a Survey

SURVEY A method of collecting a sample of data by asking people questions

SAMPLE A section of a whole group

FREQUENCY the number of time an answer is chosen Data: collection of information usually gathered by observation, questioning or measurement.

☐ **STEP 1: Plan a survey question.**

Think of a clear survey question that provides for all possibilities. This is my survey question…

_____

_____

☐ **STEP 2: Decide on a sample of data.**

Make certain the survey results are not biased by surveying people who are typical of the group of people you are interested in for example: grade 5 girls and boys. Think about how many people you will ask to take part in the survey. For my survey I am going to ask….

_____

_____

☐ **STEP 3: Conduct the survey.**

On a separate piece of paper, record people's responses to the survey. Use a tally mark to record each response.

☐ **STEP 4: Organize the data into a data table.**

After completing the survey count the tallies for each response and record the frequency in a data table.

☐ **STEP 5: Graph the data.**

Choose a type of graph to display the data.
I will display the data from the survey using a _____ graph because

_____

_____

☐ **STEP 6: Write about the results.**

On a separate piece of paper write about what you infer from your graph.

Data Survey Questions

What is Your Favourite _____ ?

- pet
- colour
- fruit
- home activity
- snack
- season
- winter activity
- summer activity
- sport
- recess activity

- pizza topping
- ice cream flavour
- dessert
- restaurant
- meal
- day of the week
- superhero
- author
- reading genre
- music genre

- school subject
- holiday
- cereal
- breakfast meal
- game
- coin
- cartoon
- lunch meal
- vegetable
- time of day

- farm animal
- dinner meal
- fast food
- movie genre
- candy
- month of the year
- weather
- country
- zoo animal
- transportation

Make Your Own Questions Related To What You Are Learning At School:

- What do you prefer?
- What do you like best?
- What is your estimation?
- What is your prediction?

More Ideas:

- How many family members are in your family?
- What colour hair do you have?
- Is your pet a mammal, reptile, bird, or fish?
- Where would you prefer to go on vacation?
- Would you rather live in the country or in the city?
- What colour eyes do you have?

- How many pets do you have?
- How many hours of sleep do you get every night?
- How many hours of TV do you watch a day?
- What would you like to be when you grow up?
- What is your birthday month?

Questions To Pose About a Graph:

- What was the most?
- What was the least?
- How many more votes does _____ have than _____?
- How many fewer votes does _____ have than _____?

- How many altogether in two categories?
- How many people were questioned in this survey?
- How many votes were there for _____?

Thinking About Misleading Graphs

Did you know some graphs can be misleading?

Favourite Orange Juice

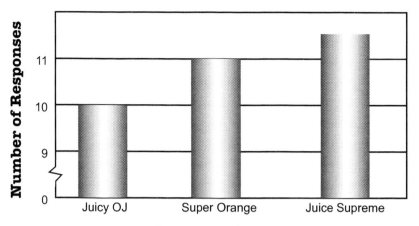

Missing Numbers

If you see a zig-zag line on the y-axis, this means that some numbers are missing from the scale. If these missing numbers were included, the bars would be closer in size.

Brain Stretch   Why are the following graphs misleading?

1. Attending the Concert

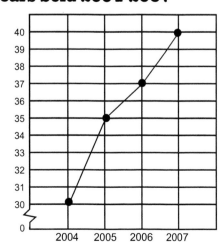

_____

_____

_____

_____

_____

2. Cars Sold 2004-2007

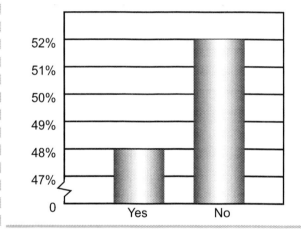

_____

_____

_____

_____

_____

Brain Stretch: Thinking About Data Management

How is data management used in every day life?

Bill's music class took a survey of students in his grade level to see which kind of music they preferred.

Here are the results:

12 Rap   4 Classical   26 Dance   18 Rock'n Roll   8 Country

Complete a tally chart to show the results.

Rap	Classical	Dance	Rock'n Roll	Country

Brain Stretch: Answer the following questions.

1. How many students took part in the survey? _____

2. What kind of music did most students prefer? _____

3. What kind of music did least students prefer? _____

4. How many more students chose dance over rap? _____

5. How many fewer students chose classical than country? _____

6. How many students chose either country or rock'n roll? _____

7. How many students chose either dance or rap? _____

8. List the music from the most preferred music to the least preferred music.

_____

TEST: Reading Data Tables

Complete.

1. Favourite Cookie

Cookie	Number
Sugar	25
Oatmeal Raisin	32
Peanut Butter	12
Chocolate Chip	14
Chocolate	58

a. What is the most popular cookie?

_____

b. How many people chose oatmeal raisin as their favorite cookie?

_____

c. How many people did not choose chocolate as their favourite cookie?

_____

2. Favourite Colour

Colour	Number
Green	12
Orange	35
Pink	9
Yellow	43
Blue	21

a. How many more people chose blue than chose pink?

_____

b. Did more people choose yellow or green?

_____

c. List the colors in order from the colour with the fewest votes to the colour with the most votes.

_____

3. Favourite Snack

Snack	Number
Yogurt	24
Raisins	12
Fruit	2
Veggies	36
Cookies	10
Ice Cream	17
Crackers	15

a. How many people chose either yogurt or ice cream?

_____

b. How many fewer people chose fruit than chose veggies?

_____

c. List the snacks in order from the snack with the fewest votes to the snack with the most votes.

_____

d. How many people were surveyed?

_____

Complete.

1. Number of Cookies Sold

Tom	🍪 🍪 🍪 🍪 🍪
Lisa	🍪 🍪 🍪 🍪 🍪 🍪 🍪
Jared	🍪 🍪 🍪
Miguel	🍪 🍪 🍪 🍪 🍪
Sarah	🍪 🍪 🍪 🍪 🍪

🍪 = 10 cookies

a. Who sold the most cookies?

_____

b. What is the range?

_____

c. How many cookies did Jared sell?

_____

d. How many more cookies did Tom sell than Sarah?

_____

e. How many cookies did Sarah sell?

_____

2. Number of Students

Grade 4	👤 👤 👤 👤 👤
Grade 5	👤 👤 👤 👤 👤 👤 👤 👤 👤
Grade 6	👤 👤 👤 👤 👤 👤
Grade 7	👤 👤 👤 👤 👤 👤 👤
Grade 8	👤 👤 👤 👤 👤 👤 👤 👤

👤 = 4 students

a. Which grade has the least number of students?

_____

b. What is the range?

_____

c. How many students in grade 4?

_____

d. How many fewer students are their in grade 6 than in grade 5?

_____

e. Which grade has 32 students?

_____

56

Name

Number of Minutes Spent on the Computer

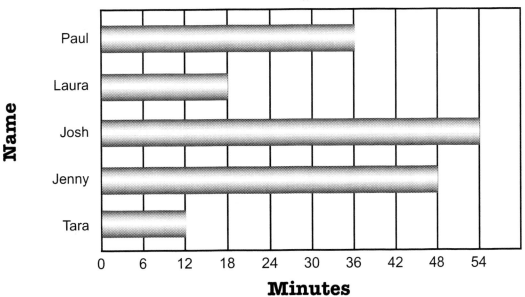

Name

Paul
Laura
Josh
Jenny
Tara

0   6   12   18   24   30   36   42   48   54

Minutes

Brain Stretch: Answer the questions.

1.	Who spent less than a half an hour on the computer?	2.	How many minutes were Paul and Tara on the computer altogether?
3.	Who was on the computer for more than three quarters of an hour?	4.	If Laura stayed on the computer for an extra 12 minutes how long would she have been on the computer?
5.	What is the range of time that was spent on the computer?	6.	Who was on the computer the longest?
7.	How many more minutes was Paul on the computer than Laura?	8.	How many fewer minutes did Tara spend on the computer than Josh?

TEST: Contructing a Bar Graph

/18

Remember Title, Labels, Scale!

Clara Brenton Public School sold magazine subscriptions to raise money for school trips. Complete a bar graph to show the number of subscriptions sold by each grade.

Data Table

Grade	Number of Magazines
Grade 1	32
Grade 2	32
Grade 3	20
Grade 4	62
Grade 5	70
Grade 6	36

Brain Stretch: Answer the questions.

1. What was the range in the number of magazines sold? _____

2. Which grade sold the most magazines? _____

3. Which grade sold the least magazines? _____

4. How many more magazines did Grade 5 sell than Grade 4? _____

5. What was the median of magazines sold? _____

6. How many magazines did grade 2 sell? _____

7. How many magazines did Grade 3 and Grade 6 sell altogether? _____

8. How many magazines were sold altogether? _____

TEST: Reading A Line Graph

Complete a line graph using the data from the table to show hockey game attendance at Oakridge Public School.

Hockey Game Attendance

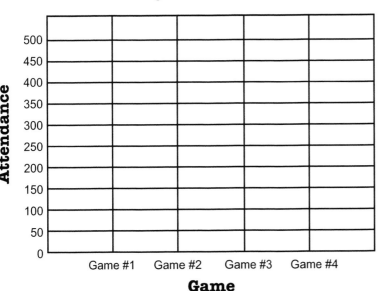

Game	# of People
Game #1	100
Game #2	350
Game #3	450
Game #4	550

Brain Stretch: Answer the following questions.

1. Which game had the most attendance? _____

2. Which game had the least attendance? _____

3. Which game(s) did not have an attendance of at least 350 people?_____

4. Which game(s) had an attendance of more than 400 people? _____

5. How many people altogether attended all four games? _____

6. Which game showed an increase of 250 people from the game before?

_____

7. By looking at the line graph, what do you notice about hockey game

attendance?_____

Complete.

1. Favourite Winter Activity

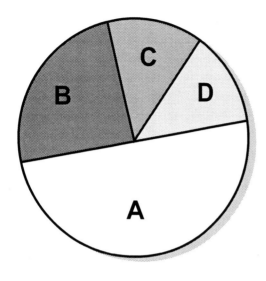

A ☐ skiing   C ▨ snowboarding
B ▦ skating   D ☐ sledding

a. What was the most popular winter activity?

_____

b. About what fraction was skating chosen?

_____

c. Which 2 winter activities together represent about ¼ of the votes?

_____

d. About what fraction was skiing?

_____

2. Favourite Type of Presents

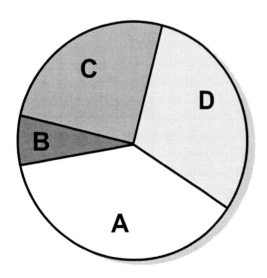

A ☐ Clothes   C ▨ Video games
B ▦ CDs   D ☐ Money

a. What was the least popular type of present?

_____

b. About what fraction was clothes?

_____

c. Which 2 types of presents together represent about 1/3 of the votes?

_____

d. About what fraction was money?

_____

Complete.

1. Favourite Type of Reading Material

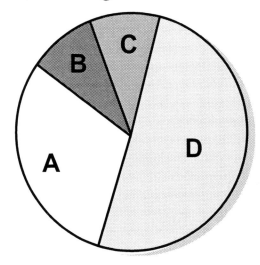

A ☐ Mystery 29%   C ▨ Magazine 10%

B ▨ Non-Fiction 9%   D ☐ Fiction 52%

a. The percent of votes for mystery is about how many times the number of votes for magazines?

_____

b. What is the ratio of fiction to non-fiction?

_____

c. What is the ratio of magazines to fiction?

_____

d. What was the percent of votes for either non-fiction or magazines?

_____

2. Number of Books Read in a Month

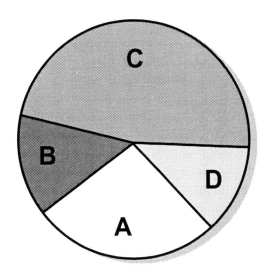

A ☐ 2 books 24%   C ▨ 3 books 45%

B ▨ 5 books 17%   D ☐ 4 books 14%

a. What percentage was 2 books?

_____

b. What fraction of students read 3 books?

_____

c. What is the ratio of 5 books to 2 books?

_____

d. If 200 students were surveyed, how many students read exactly 4 books?

_____

TEST: Stem-and-Leaf Plots

Answer the questions.

1. Find the mode of the data.

Stem	Leaves
0	5 2
1	5 5
2	8

mode _____

2. Find the range of the data.

Stem	Leaves
1	0 6 4 6
2	6
3	2 2 4 6 6
4	
5	
6	7

range _____

3. Find the mean of the data.

Stem	Leaves
12	4
13	3
14	
15	7 5 4

mean _____

4. Find the median of the data.

Stem	Leaves
64	1 7 1 8
65	2 9 6 8 5
66	8
67	6 8 7 0

median _____

5. Find the median of the data.

Stem	Leaves
15	0 6 9
16	3 4 8

median _____

6. Find the range of the data.

Stem	Leaves
6	9 1
7	4 8 0
8	3 3

range _____

7. Find the mean of the data.

Stem	Leaves
53	7
54	7 4 8
55	6 4
56	2
57	6
58	9

mean _____

8. Find the mode of the data.

Stem	Leaves
1	7 6 9
2	1 0
3	
4	2 0 1

mode _____

Data Management Test #1

Complete the chart.   Name _____

#	Set of Data	Mean	Range	Median	Mode
1.	28, 21, 3, 10, 6, 9, and 21				
2.	24, 3, 17, 23, 19, 19, and 7				
3.	13, 4, 9, 23, 24, and 23				
4.	12, 21, 12, 7, and 8				
5.	7, 19, 28, 8, and 28				

Data Management Test #2

Complete the chart.   Name _____

#	Set of Data	Mean	Range	Median	Mode
1.	5, 25, 14, 25, 25, 2, and 2				
2.	7, 6, 2, 6, 28, 4, and 10				
3.	15, 27, 28, 5, and 5				
4.	22, 25, 17, 22, and 4				
5.	7, 28, 7, 6, and 7				

Constructing A Graph

This data table shows information about the favourite subjects of Mr. Turnbull's class. Construct a graph to show the results. Make sure you label your graph!

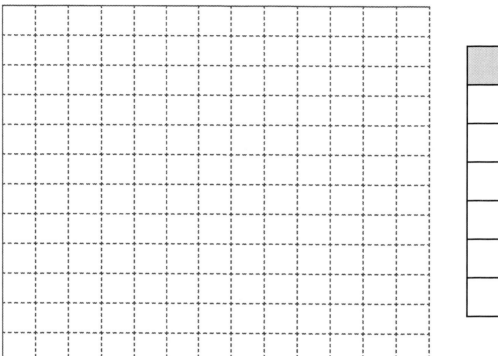

Brain Stretch: Answer the questions.

Write about what you learned from the graph.

_____

_____

_____

_____

What kind of graph did you choose to display the data? Explain your thinking.

_____

_____

_____

Constructing a Line Graph

Here is a table to show _____

_____

Complete and label a line graph to show the data.

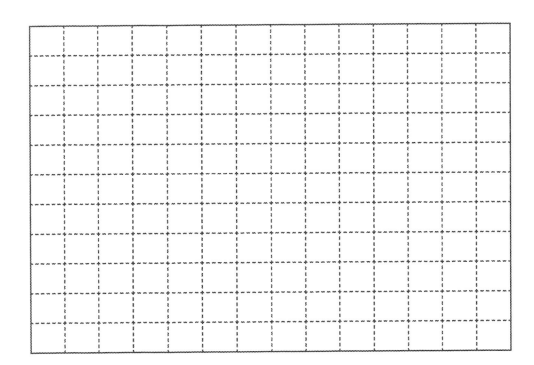

Brain Stretch:

On a separate piece of paper, write about what information you have learned from your line graph.

Constructing a Double Bar Graph

Here is a table to show _____

_____

A. Complete and label a double bar graph to show the data.

Brain Stretch: What can you infer from the graph?

1. _____

2. _____

3. _____

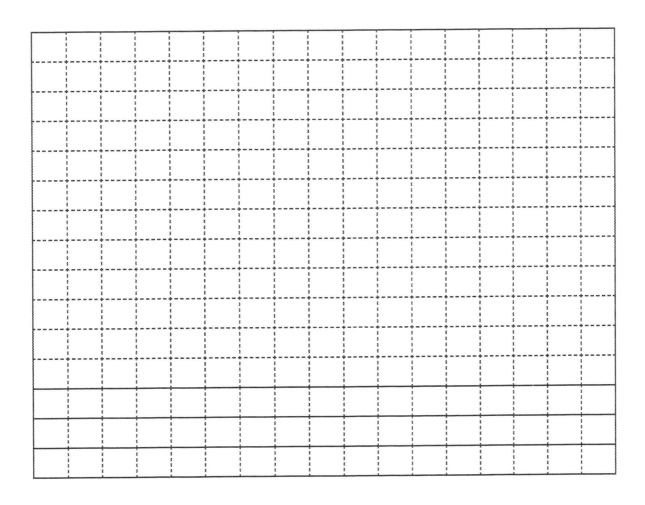

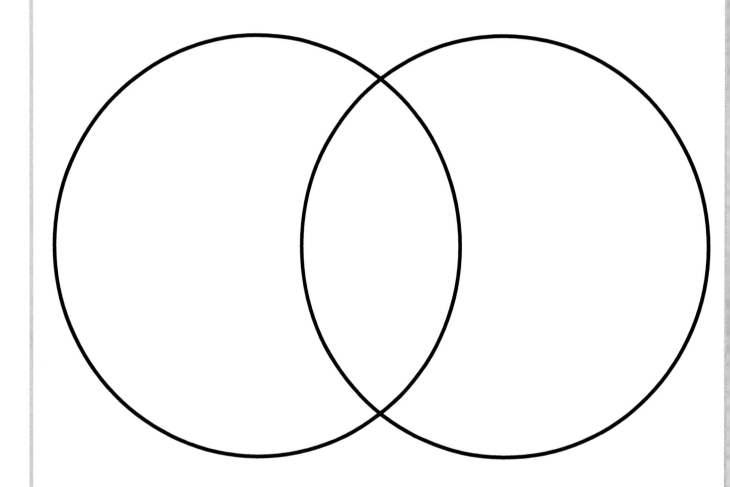

Venn Diagram

1. Sort factors into the Venn Diagram, using the rules listed below.

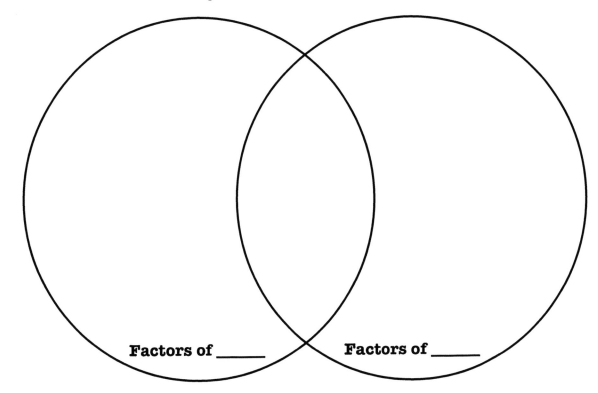

Factors of _____   **Factors of _____**

2. Sort factors into the Venn Diagram, using the rules listed below.

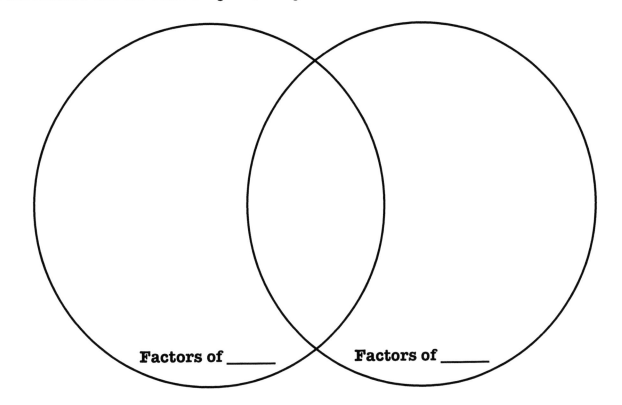

Factors of _____   **Factors of _____**

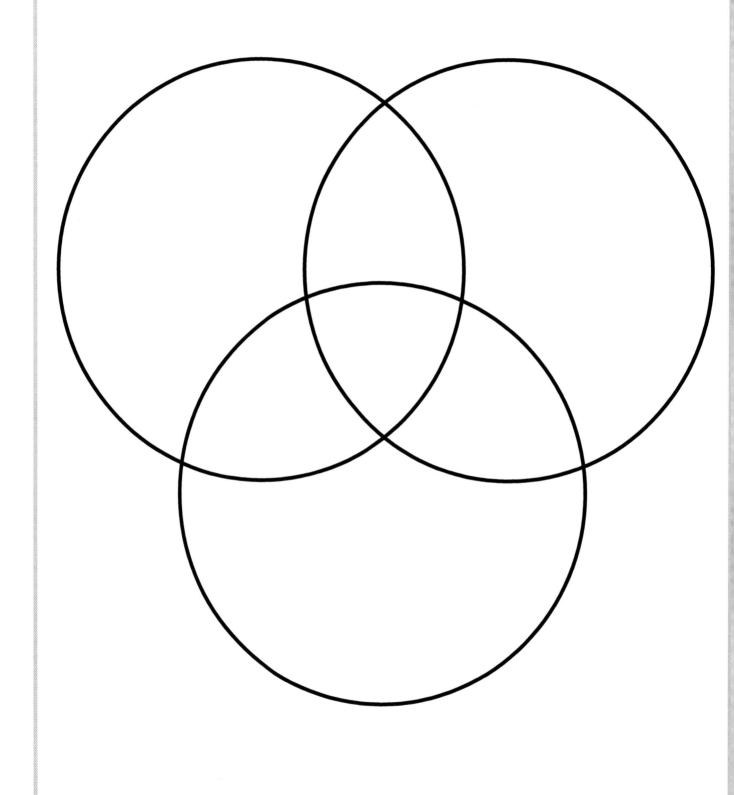

Daily Math Work Rubric

Student _____

	Level 1	Level 2	Level 3	Level 4
Understanding of Math Concepts	Student demonstrates a limited understanding of math concepts in daily work.	Student demonstrates a satisfactory understanding of skills in daily work.	Student demonstrates a complete understanding of math concepts in daily work details.	Student demonstrates a thorough understanding of math concepts in daily work.
Application of Skills Taught	Student rarely applies skills taught in daily work without teacher assistance.	Student applies skills taught in daily work with several errors and omissions.	Student applies skills taught in daily work with few errors and omissions.	Student consistently applies skills taught in daily work with almost no errors and omissions.
Math Terminology	Student rarely uses appropriate math terms during math discussions and activities.	Student sometimes uses appropriate math terms during math discussions and activities.	Student usually uses appropriate math terms during math discussions and activities.	Student consistently uses appropriate math terms during math discussions and activities.
Ready For Class	Student rarely comes prepared with materials and assignments done.	Student sometimes comes prepared with materials and assignments done.	Student usually comes prepared with materials and assignments done.	Student consistently comes prepared with materials and assignments done.
Use of Class Time	Student needs frequent reminders to use time wisely.	Student needs some reminders to use time wisely.	Student needs few reminders to use time wisely.	Student rarely needs reminders to use time wisely.

Additional Observations

_____

_____

Grade 4 Data Management

Student _____

Expectation	Level 1 Not Yet	Level 2 Developing	Level 3 Proficient	Level 4 Mastered
read, describe, and interpret primary data and secondary data presented in charts and graphs, including stem-and-leaf plots and double bar graphs				
read, interpret, and draw conclusions from primary data				
compare similarities and differences between two related sets of data				
collect data by conducting a survey or an experiment to do with themselves, their environment, issues in their school or the community, or content from another subject and record observations or measurements				
collect and organize discrete primary data and display data in charts, table and graphs, that have appropriate titles, labels and scales that suit the range and distribution of data, using a variety of tools				
demonstrate through investigation the value of median and determine the median of a set of data				

Level 1 - Student rarely applies skills with several errors or omissions.

Level 2 - Student sometimes applies skills with some errors or omissions.

Level 3 - Student usually applies skills with few errors or omissions.

Level 4 - Student consistently applies skills with almost no errors or omissions.

Grade 5 Data Management

Student _____

Expectation	Level 1 Not Yet	Level 2 Developing	Level 3 Proficient	Level 4 Mastered
distinguish between discrete data and continuous data				
collect data by conducting a survey or an experiment to do with themselves, their environment, issues in their school or community, or content from another subject, and record observations or measurements				
collect and organize discrete or continuous primary data and secondary data and display the data in charts, graphs or tables that have appropriate titles, labels and scales that suit the range and distribution of the data, using a variety of tools				
demonstrate an understanding that sets of data can be samples of larger populations				
Describe, through investigation, how a set of data is collected and explain whether the collection method is appropriate				
read, interpret, and draw conclusions from primary data				
compare similarities and differences between two related sets of data, using a variety of strategies				
calculate the mean for a small set of data and sue it to describe the shape of the data set across its range of values, using charts, tables and graphs				

Level 1 - Student rarely applies skills with several errors or omissions.

Level 2 - Student sometimes applies skills with some errors or omissions.

Level 3 - Student usually applies skills with few errors or omissions.

Level 4 - Student consistently applies skills with almost no errors or omissions.

Grade 6 Data Management

Student _____

Expectation	Level 1 Not Yet	Level 2 Developing	Level 3 Proficient	Level 4 Mastered
collect data by conducting a survey or an experiment to do with themselves, their environment, issues in their school or community, content from another subject, and record observations or measurements				
collect and organize discrete or continuous primary data and secondary data and display the data in charts, tables and graphs that have appropriate titles, labels and scales				
read, describe, and interpret data, and explain relationships between sets of data				
select an appropriate type of graph to represent a set of data, graph the data using technology, and justify the choice of graph				
determine through investigation, how well a set of data represents a population, on the basis of the method that was used to collect the data				
read, interpret, and draw conclusions from primary data and from secondary data				
explain how different scales used on graphs can influence conclusions drawn from the data				
demonstrate an understanding of mean				

Level 1 - Student rarely applies skills with several errors or omissions.

Level 2 - Student sometimes applies skills with some errors or omissions.

Level 3 - Student usually applies skills with few errors or omissions.

Level 4 - Student consistently applies skills with almost no errors or omissions.

KEEP UP THE GREAT WORK!

STUDENT: _____

DATA MANAGEMENT EXPERT!

STUDENT: _____

ANSWER KEY

PAGE #	ANSWER KEY
2	Part A Number 11, 12, 4, 6, 8. 1. 16 2. 5 3. 19 4. carrots Part B Number 7, 3, 8, 5, 9 1. 12 2. 3 3. 2 4. baseball
3	Part A Number 11, 15, 8, 12, 4 1. 26 2. 8 3. 8 4. white milk Part B Number 9, 2, 13, 10, 9 1. 15 2. 1 3. 17 4. 43
4	1. 104 2. Fiction and Mystery 2. Poetry 4. 19 5. 25 6. 60 7. Fiction and Mystery 8. Poetry, Sci-Fiction, Non Fiction, Mystery or Fiction
5	1. a. 7 b. Grapes c. 4 2. a. Spring b. Summer c. Summer, Winter, Fall, Spring 3. a. Monday b. Wednesday and Friday c. 8 d. Sunday and Tuesday
6	1. 7cm 2. 10.43cm 3. 6cm 4. 13cm 5. #6 6. 10cm 7. #4 8. none 9. #1, #3, #5 10. #1 and #2
7	1. $22 2. $318 3. $20 4. April 5. $625 6. $1849
8	1. 93 2. 8 or 13 3. 71 4. 32 5. 8 6. 12
9	1. 118 2. 32 3. Gr. 6 and Gr. 1 4. Gr. 3 5. double bar graph, answers may vary 6. increase for all grades
10	1. 134 2. a. 13 b. 16 3. 113 4. 20 5. 2 6. 3
11	1. 205 2. Kaitlyn 3. Michael 4. Spencer and Megan 5. 65 6. 15 7. 5 8. 20 9. Ben 10. 35
12	1. 93 2. Hockey 3. Baseball 4. 18 5. 15 6. 45 7. 9 8. 8 9. 27 10. Baseball, Basketball, Soccer, Hockey
13	1. Strawberry 2. Chocolate 3. 40 4. 20 5. 84 6. 20 7. 24 8. 44:24 or 11:6 9. 40:20 or 2:1 10. 128
14	1.a. John b. 40 mins c. 24 mins. d. 6 e. 32 mins 2.a. January b. 55 c. 25 d. May e. 20
15	1. Bicycle 2. Other 3. 12 4. Bicycle 5. 52 6. 8 7. Other, School Bus, Car, Walk, Bicycle
16	1. 1 2. Black 3. 4 4. 30 5. 11 6. 6 7. 43 8. Black, Silver, Red, Blue

PAGE #	ANSWER KEY
17	1. Red 2. 26 3. 16 4. 5 5. 9 6. 49 7. Green, Black, Orange, Red 8. 18
18	1. 172 2. Country 3. Rock and Roll 4. 4 5. Country 6. 72 7. 53 8. Rock and Roll, Classical, Other, Rap, Country
19	1. Eric 2. Sean, James, Julia, Alex 3. 40 4. 20 5. 80 6. Sean 7. Eric, Olivia, Tara, Kate, James, Julia, Alex, Sean 8. Tara
20	1. Shelley, $80 2. $40 3. $40 4. $10 5. $145 6. John 7. John, Rob, Vicky, Shelley 8. $65
21	1. E 2. 24 3. D 4. 24 5. E, A, C, B, D 6. 2 classes
22	Answers will vary
23	1. 445 2. Wednesday 3. 25 4. 55 5. 35 6. Mark 7. 30 8. Friday 9. 20 10. 25
24	1. 140 2. 5 3. 5 4. 5 5. 15 6. 70 7. 70 8. Orange and Yellow 9. Red 10. White
25	1. 115 2. 25 3. 10 4. 35 5. Tuesday 6. Chocolate 7. 10 8. Wednesday 9. Monday 10. 240
26	1. No 2. 24:30 or 4:5 3. Answers will vary
27	Answers will vary
28	1. a. 12cm b. April c. 14 cm d. 14 cm e. 18 cm 2. a. 12 cm b. 2 cm c. 14 cm d. 14 cm e. 4 cm
29	Attendance: 175, 100, 125, 225 1. Saturday 2. Thursday 3. Thursday 4. 100 5. 125 6. Answers will vary
30	1. week 6 2. 2 cm 3. week 2 4. 10 cm 5. 10 cm 6. 2 cm increase each week
31	1. May 2. 16 degrees 3. 16 degrees 4. 28 degrees 5. 2 degrees 6. increase
32	1. Chickens 2. 1/4 3. 1/2 4. pigs and ducks

ANSWER KEY

PAGE #	ANSWER KEY
33	1. Rap and Classical 2. Country 3. 1/3 4. Rap and Classical, Rock and Roll, Country
34	1. 52/100 or 26/50 or 13/25 2. 104 3. 36 4. 52 5. 22/100 or 11/50 6. 16
35	1. 1/5 or 20/100 or 2/10 or 1/5 2. 36:21 or 12:7 3. 28 4. 43 5. Baseball 6. Tennis, Gymnastics, Soccer, Baseball
36	1. 2 pets 2. 18:16 or 9:8 3. 15% 4. 33% 5. 31% 6. 18/100 or 9/50
37	1. Drive 2. 12:22 3. School Bus 4. 2% 5. 66% 6. 12/100 or 6/50 or 2/25
38	1. 18 2. 21 3. 21 4. 5 5. 21 6. 26 7. 24 8. 13 9. 25 10. 14 11. 19 12. 21 13. 11 14. 12 15. 20 16. 26 17. 13 18. 19 19. 10 20. 25
39	1. 24 2. 25 3. 17 4. 13 5. 24 6. 16 7. 20 8. 17 9. 14 10. 26 11. 17 12. 7 13. 16 14. 23 15. 13 16. 21 17. 17 18. 23 19. 26 20. 18
40	1. 17 2. 13 3. 11 4. 15 5. 12 6. 20 7. 15 8. 11
41	1. 13 2. 23 3. 15 4. 15 5. 15 6. 11 7. 17 8. 9
42	1. Mean 12 Median 13 Mode No mode 2. Mean 11 Median 7 Mode 7 3. Mean 20 Median 22.5 Mode 12 and 25 4. Mean 20 Median 18 Mode 18 5. Mean 10 Median 6 Mode 6 6. Mean 9 Median 6 Mode 6 7. Mean 6 Median 5.5 Mode 5 and 6 8. Mean 15 Median 18 Mode 18 9. Mean 12 Median 9.5 Mode 8 10. Mean 4 Median 4 Mode 2 and 4
43	1. Factors of 72: 1, 2, 3, 4, 6, 8, 9, 12, 18, 24, 36, 72 Factors of 81: 1, 3, 9, 27, 81 2. Factors of 64: 1, 2, 4, 8, 16, 32, 64 Factors of 48: 1, 2, 3, 4, 6, 8, 12, 16, 24, 48
44	1. Factors of 45: 1, 5, 9, 45 Factors of 36: 1, 2, 3, 4, 6, 9, 12, 18, 36 2. Factors of 54: 1, 2, 3, 6, 9, 18, 27, 54 Factors of 42: 1, 2, 3, 6, 7, 14, 21, 42
45	1. no mode 2. 58 3. 33 4. 41 5. 33 6. 39 7. no mode 8. 34.5

ANSWER KEY

PAGE #	ANSWER KEY
46	1. 50 2. 331 3. 76 4. 18 5. 141 6. 73 7. 20 8. 16
47	1. 45 2. 52 3. 162 and 171 4. 12, 24, 28, 72 5. 257 6. 9 7. 41 8. 71
49	1. Bar Graph or Picto 2. Circle Graph 3. Double Bar Graph 4. Double Bar Graph 5. Bar Graph or Picto 6. Line Graph 7. Line Graph 8. Bar Graph or Picto 9. Bar Graph or Picto 10. Bar Graph 11. Circle Graph 12. Line Graph
52	Answers will vary
53	Answers will vary
54	1. 68 2. Dance 3. Classical 4. 14 5. 4 6. 26 7. 38 8. Dance, Rock and Roll, Rap, Country, Classical
55	1. a. Chocolate b. 32 c. 83 2. a. 12b. Yellow c. Pink, Green, Blue, Orange, Yellow 3. a. 41 b. 34 c. Fruit, Cookies, Raisins, Crackers, Ice Cream, Yogurt, Veggies d. 116
56	1. a. Lisa b. 40 c. 30 d. 5 e. 45 2. a. Grade 4 b. 14 c. 18 d. 10 e. Grade 5 and Grade 8
57	1. Laura and Tara 2. 48 mins 3. Jenny and Josh 4. 30 mins 5. 42 mins 6. Josh 7. 18 mins 8. 42 mins
58	1. 50 2. Grade 5 3. Grade 3 4. 8 5. 42 6. 32 7. 56 8. 252
59	1. Game 4 2. Game 1 3. Game 1 4. Game 3 and 4 5. 1450 6. Game 2 7. increase with each game
60	1. a. skiing b. 1/4 c. snow boarding and sledding d. 1/2 2. a. CDs b. 1/3 c. Video Games and CDs d. 1/3
61	1. a. 3 times b. 52:9 c. 10:52 d. 19% 2. a. 24% b. 45/100 or 9/20 c. 17:24 d. 28
62	1. 15 2. 57 3. 144.6 4. 657 5. 161 6. 22 7. 557 8. no mode

PAGE #	ANSWER KEY

#	Set of Data	Mean	Range	Median	Mode
1.	28, 21, 3, 10, 6, 9, and 21	14	25	10	21
2.	24, 3, 17, 23, 19, 19, and 7	16	21	19	19
3.	13, 4, 9, 23, 24, and 23	16	20	18	23
4.	12, 21, 12, 7, and 8	12	14	12	12
5.	7, 19, 28, 8, and 28	18	21	19	28

63

#	Set of Data	Mean	Range	Median	Mode
1.	5, 25, 14, 25, 25, 2, and 2	14	23	14	25
2.	7, 6, 2, 6, 28, 4, and 10	9	26	6	6
3.	15, 27, 28, 5, and 5	16	23	15	5
4.	22, 25, 17, 22, and 4	18	21	22	22
5.	7, 28, 7, 6, and 7	11	22	7	7